TO_____

FROM_____

ON THE OCCASION OF_____

DATE_____

Bible words about

Happiness

for Children

retold by

Lois Rock

illustrated by

Claire Henley

CP

Text by Lois Rock
Copyright © 1996 Lion Publishing
Illustrations copyright © 1996 Claire Henley

The author asserts the moral right
to be identified as the author of this work

Published by
Lion Publishing plc
Sandy Lane West, Oxford, England
ISBN 0 7459 3345 9
Lion Publishing
4050 Lee Vance View, Colorado Springs,
CO 80918, USA
ISBN 0 7459 3345 9
Albatross Books Pty Ltd
PO Box 320, Sutherland, NSW 2232, Australia
ISBN 0 7324 1300 1

First edition 1996

Acknowledgments
Bible quotations are taken from the *Good News Bible*,
copyright © American Bible Society, New York,
1966, 1971 and 4th edition 1976, published by the
Bible Societies/HarperCollins, with permission

A catalogue record for this book is available
from the British Library

Library of Congress CIP Data applied for

Printed and bound in Singapore

Bible words about Happiness

In the beginning, the Bible says, God made the world and everything in it. It was a good and safe place, where people were happy. They had all they needed. They were friends with one another. Best of all, they were friends with God.

Then people made a big mistake. They disobeyed God. Everything went wrong!

Two thousand years ago, the Bible says, God came to the world as a person—Jesus—to put things right. He told people not to worry about trying to buy themselves lots of nice things. He told them not to be afraid of hard times. 'Set your heart on being God's friend,' said Jesus. 'And live as God wants. God will keep you safe. And you will be truly happy for ever: "blessed".'

You can read what Jesus said about happiness in the Bible book called Matthew, chapter 5, verses 3 to 12.

Happy are those who know they don't deserve to be God's friends.

It's so easy to do wrong things. Then you feel sad and ashamed.

Here's surprising news to make you happy:
you are welcome as a child in God's family just as you are.

Dear God
I know I do wrong things.
I am sorry.
But I'm really happy to know that you welcome me.

Happy are those who feel so sad they want to cry and cry.

Sometimes it seems that everything's gone wrong. Nothing in the world can make things right.

But here's good news: God is with you. God is in charge of the problem. God will comfort you.

Dear God
Knowing that you are
with me
in the sad times
is a bit like knowing there
is a sun
behind the clouds.
How happy I am
to know you're there.

Happy are those who don't push to get their own way.

Sometimes it's hard to put other people first. What if you miss out on good things?

But wait: here's some important news. God notices those who put other people first, God loves them and promises to give them good things.

Dear God
It's not easy to stand back while others help themselves.
Help me to trust in your promises.
I know you will make me happy.

Happy are those who long to do what God wants.

There are so many things you dream of doing! But the best thing of all is finding out for yourself how good and loving and kind God is; learning to be good and kind and loving to others.

Here's cheering news: God will help you to do all of those things.

Dear God
With your help
I can be the kind of person
you want me to be.
I can be the kind of person
I really want to be.
And that will make me
happy.

Happy are those who forgive others.

How good it is
to be forgiven.

Here's great news:
God will forgive you
in the same way
that you forgive
others.

Dear God
You forgive me.
You rub out all my
mistakes.
You give me a fresh new
start
and make me glad.

Happy are those who love what is good and right.

If good things make you cheer,
if you are truly glad when right beats wrong,
here's the best news yet:

One day you will really see God who is good in every way.

Dear God
In the good things of this world
I glimpse your perfect goodness.
How happy I am to think that one day
I will see you more clearly,
I will meet you face to face.

Happy are those who work for peace.

Will quarrels ever end? Will fighting ever stop?

Here's amazing news: if you try to bring peace where there were quarrels then you are God's child, part of God's family.

Dear God
I know that quarrels hurt.
I want a world full of peace and love.
I want to be your child.

Happy are those who suffer hard times because they do what God wants.

Who can feel happy when they have tried to be kind and others only hurt them?

Here's good news for the bad times: God is close to you. You are not alone. You belong to God.

Dear God
I want to live as your friend and to be kind.
Please let me know you are close
when other people hurt me,
and keep me joyful.

Happy are you when people tease you and bully you and tell lies about you for following Jesus.

It's not nice being teased and bullied. And it's not fair!

Here's news to remember: the people who live as God's friends always get into trouble for it. But some day, God will put everything right.

Dear God
I will live as your friend.
I will wait bravely
for the time
when you put an end to
bad things
and you give me
the good things
you have kept for me.

Love your enemies.
Do good to those who
hate you.

God has made the sun and rain and God gives these good things to everyone— good and bad alike. And those who want to live as God's friends and enjoy the happiness that God gives must do good and kind things to everyone— good and bad alike.

Dear God
You show me the way
that leads to happiness—
the way that leads me
to you,
to where I can be
your child.
You will give me
good things
for ever.

◇Happy are those who know they don't deserve to be God's friends.

◇Happy are those who feel so sad they want to cry and cry.

◇Happy are those who don't push to get their own way.

◇Happy are those who long to do what God wants.

◇Happy are those who forgive others.

◇Happy are those who love what is good and right.

◇Happy are those who work for peace.

◇Happy are those who suffer hard times because they do what God wants.

◇Happy are you when people tease you and bully you and tell lies about you for following Jesus.

◆Love your enemies. Do good to those who hate you.

◇ *Happy are those who know they are spiritually poor; the Kingdom of heaven belongs to them!*

◇ *Happy are those who mourn; God will comfort them!*

◇ *Happy are those who are humble; they will receive what God has promised.*

◇ *Happy are those whose greatest desire is to do what God requires; God will satisfy them fully!*

◇ *Happy are those who are merciful to others; God will be merciful to them!*

◇ *Happy are the pure in heart; they will see God!*

◇ *Happy are those who work for peace; God will call them his children!*

◇ *Happy are those who are persecuted because they do what God requires; the Kingdom of heaven belongs to them!*

◇ *Happy are you when people insult you and persecute you and tell all kinds of evil lies against you because you are my followers. Be happy and glad, for a great reward is kept for you in heaven.*

◆ *You have heard that it was said, 'Love your friends, hate your enemies.' But now I tell you: love your enemies and pray for those who persecute you, so that you may become the sons of your Father in heaven. For he makes his sun to shine on bad and good people alike, and gives rain to those who do good and to those who do evil.*